The Forward Book
of Poetry 1998

FORWARD PUBLISHING
LONDON

First published in Great Britain by
Forward Publishing · 84-86 Regent Street · London W1R 6DD
in association with
Faber and Faber · 3 Queen Square · London WC1N 3AU

ISBN 0 571 19286 6 (paperback)

Compilation copyright © Forward Publishing 1997
For copyright on individual poems see acknowledgements page 7
Foreword copyright © John Fuller 1997
Front cover illustration by Kate Whiteford

Reprographics by Colour Path
Soho · London

Printed by Redwood Books Ltd.
Kennet House · Kennet Way · Trowbridge · Wilts. BA14 8RN

A CIP catalogue reference for this book
is available at the British Library.

To Maude

Preface

WELCOME TO THE SIXTH FORWARD BOOK OF POETRY. The poems in this anthology are culled from the hundreds of collections and the many individual poems published throughout the year in Britain.

As always the judges have sifted carefully and conscientiously to make this selection and I'd like to thank them for a discerning read.

As is now our tradition, *The Forward Book of Poetry* is published on National Poetry Day, our fourth annual celebration of poetry throughout the British Isles. Hundreds of poetic events will be taking place, poem cards will be distributed in supermarkets, and through the BBC's extensive network of national and local television and radio, poems will fill the airwaves.

I'd like to thank the many poetry commandos who have energetically made this possible: Gordon Kerr at Waterstone's, Jeffery Tolman at Tolman Cunard and everyone at the BBC, The Poetry Society, Colman Getty and Forward Publishing.

And finally thank you to the John S Cohen Foundation, which has paid to have this anthology distributed to Britain's hospitals and prisons. May it bring comfort and companionship to all readers in need.

William Sieghart

Foreword

WHAT A WORLD THIS BOOK OFFERS! That's the way it is with an
anthology (its etymology a gathering of flowers, a vased bunch you
never found looking quite like that in a mere garden). But admire the
variety of these cut blooms: a flattened wedding-ring, a deer on the
road, a sexual artichoke, the corset lady, the shrinking father, a Lady
Judge suckling her child in court, the burden of beauty, the secrets of
the elbow, the source of the Thames as a symbol of the fragility of
memory, a shape-changing revenge on a voyeur, the *deus absconditus* as a
Gallic idler, etcetera. If it is in the nature of poems to surprise and
delight, then this selection will surely do so.

This anthology is a late stage in a long process. When the
accumulation of over 5,000 of the year's submitted poems arrived, the
five judges got down to five weeks of reading them and then met for five
hours to argue out their shortlists. If this sounds as hopeless as the
Walrus's seven maids with seven mops, rest assured this annual process
actually works. The daunting pile began to yield its riches. The judges
met with unjaded enthusiasm. Divergent tastes were accommodated,
and where there was something less than universal acclamation, voting
seemed to secure a fair result. Even lunch had to compete with
our desire to go on reading the poems to each other, to enthuse, to
persuade, to distinguish, to prefer, while forks lay idle.

We all found the Best Collection shortlist the hardest to distil.
I'm sure that my personal difficulties were entirely characteristic: of the
eighty-four volumes submitted in this category, I found twenty-three
that I would have loved to recommend to readers by including them,
and of these I thought eleven could not possibly disgrace a shortlist of
the highest calibre, none indeed unworthy of the prize. While regretting
the necessary omission of many admired and loved names, we think
that our full shortlist of six is a strong one, varied in every way. And we
think that the other shortlists, identifying the most promising new

voices and the most striking poems in periodicals (grace to those editors who still find space), are strong too, and representative of those qualities we found ourselves most valuing everywhere: controlled passion and energetic thought; ability to shape and dramatise the individual poem; concern for the human subject sculpted in necessary language. Alas, neither obsessive emotion nor mere eloquence can guarantee a good poem. Wisdom, wit, verbal inventiveness: these are as nothing without the vision of the poem itself which shapes the skills that go to make it. In the light of the central poetic imagination, poetry is not a competition but a shared gift. We were all the time aware that the act of judicial selection should never be also an exclusion: if we have opened a door and beckoned some through, that door still remains open.

Geordie Greig, Kathleen Jamie, Chris Meade, Sue Roberts and myself have much enjoyed the work we have put into this anthology, and we look forward to the no less difficult responsibility of choosing the winners in each category. We salute the generous vision of William Sieghart of Forward Publishing, and are much indebted to the discreet and patient guidance of Liz Sich and Margot Weale at Colman Getty. The Forward Prize is now a major institution, and the proselytizing work that it does for poetry is invaluable.

Most poetry eventually joins the vast shelves of the unread and most readers of poetry follow a beaten track. Time, which is said to be the mother of truth, can all too easily confirm habit and lay its slow dust on the unclamorous. The present anthology is an attempt to counter this, and to make more time for poetry. It offers signposts for other routes and maps against oblivion. Take it as a guide and a sampler. Our collective sense of humility as judges was continually bolstered by our excitement as readers. You above all, reader, must also be active in your discrimination. Which of the shortlisted work do you think should have won? And which of the collections will you buy?

John Fuller

Acknowledgements

John Agard · MILLENNIUM BUG · *From the Devil's Pulpit* · Bloodaxe Books

Gillian Allnutt · THE GARDEN IN ESH WINNING · *Nantucket and the Angel* ·
    Bloodaxe Books

Moniza Alvi · THE JOB · *Poetry Review*

A R Ammons · HOW THINGS GO WRONG · *Brink Road* · WW Norton

Simon Armitage · THE TYRE · *Cloud Cuckoo Land* · Faber and Faber

Phil Bowen · WHAT A LITTLE SCARECROW CAN DO · *Variety's Hammer* · Stride

John Burnside · PENITENCE · *A Normal Skin* · Cape Poetry

Harry Clifton · GOD IN FRANCE · Poetry Review

Stephen Dobyns · COLD MARBLE · *Common Carnage* · Bloodaxe Books

Jane Draycott · ELBOW · THE PRINCE RUPERT'S DROP · *No Theatre* ·
    Smith/Doorstop Books

Helen Dunmore · THE GETHSEMANE GARDEN COMPETITION · *Bestiary* ·
    Bloodaxe Books

Ruth Fainlight · THE CORSET LADY · *Sugar-Paper Blue* · Bloodaxe Books

Peter Finch · ALL I NEED IS THREE PLUMS · *Useful* · Seren

Linda France · HER DOGNESS · *Storyville* · Bloodaxe Books

Matthew Francis · A BLIND MAN IN THE FOREST · POEM WITHOUT WORDS ·
    Blizzard · Faber and Faber

Lavinia Greenlaw · A WORLD WHERE NEWS TRAVELLED SLOWLY ·
    Times Literary Supplement

David Harsent · THE MAKERS · London Review of Books

W N Herbert · THE WIVES OF WEINSBERG · Verse Vol 13, no 1

Tracey Herd · INDIAN SUMMER · THE SIEGE · *No Hiding Place* · Bloodaxe Books

Selima Hill · MY WEDDING RING · PLEASE CAN I HAVE A MAN · *Violet* ·
    Bloodaxe Books

Jane Holland · THEY ARE A TABLEAU AT THE KISSING-GATE · *The Brief History of
    a Disreputable Woman* · Bloodaxe Books

Ted Hughes · ACTAEON · *Tales from Ovid* · Faber and Faber

Ted Hughes · PLATFORM ONE · The Sunday Times

Fred Johnston · MUSIC · *True North* · Salmon Poetry

Stephen Knight · THE SURF MOTEL · *Dream City Cinema* · Bloodaxe Books

Roddy Lumsden · FIN · YEAH YEAH YEAH · *Yeah Yeah Yeah* · Bloodaxe Books

Sarah Maguire · THE INVISIBLE MENDER (MY FIRST MOTHER) ·

   The Invisible Mender · Cape Poetry

Jamie McKendrick · ANCIENT HISTORY · BONESHAKER · *The Marble Fly* ·

   Oxford University Press

Andrew Motion · FRESH WATER · *Salt Water* · Faber and Faber

Dennis O'Driscoll · FAITH, HOPE, LOSS · *Quality Time* · Anvil Press Poetry

Don Paterson · A PRIVATE BOTTLING · *God's Gift to Women* · Faber and Faber

Brian Patten · THE ARMADA · *Armada* · Flamingo

Katrina Porteous · WRECKED CREEVES · *The Lost Music* · Bloodaxe Books

Peter Porter · THE WESTERN CANOE · *Dragons in their Pleasant Palaces* ·

   Oxford University Press

Craig Raine · RASHOMON: THE OPERA · The Sunday Times

Peter Redgrove · RELAXATION EXERCISES · *Orchard End* · Stride

Robin Robertson · ARTICHOKE · ESCAPOLOGY · *A Painted Field* · Picador

Carol Rumens · A DAY IN THE LIFE OF FARMER DREAM · Tabla Issue 6

Eva Salzman · TREPANNED · *Bargain with the Watchman* · Oxford University Press

Ruth Silcock · THE ELOCUTION LESSON · *A Wonderful View of the Sea* · Anvil Press

Susan Wicks · MY FATHER IS SHRINKING · ON RE-RECORDING MOZART ·

   The Clever Daughter · Faber and Faber

C K Williams · INSIGHT · *The Vigil* · Bloodaxe Books

Benjamin Zephaniah · THE ANGRY BLACK POET · *Propa Propaganda* ·

   Bloodaxe Books

Contents

The Best Collection Poems

Selima Hill

My Wedding Ring

I hammered it out like a palette-knife,
flat, for a minnow,
(you wouldn't get that)
or a shrunken platinum plaque
with your love message still engraved on it
in barely-visible loops
as if the dried bodies of sea-horses
had journeyed from a sea
you couldn't even look at without swimming in
it was so blue –
and now you say you don't know what I mean.
I'm not surprised after last night.
I've never been so close to another woman,
a woman brimming over with the details
my 'real' friends were kind enough to spare me,
brimming over like the sandwich box
of maddened wasps
you left on the cooker that night
till the plastic started to melt
and stick to their wings,
and I scraped the whole singed tangle into the sink,
and some of them were trying to clamber out –
and I'm trying not to post you back your ring,
make a little parcel of it for you,
tissue-paper, bows, a little note.
But what's the use? You wouldn't understand.
I might just as well post you
this sudden undignified craving
for tinned milk
I keep giving in to, and sucking,
like *Who shall I cling to,*
who shall I cling to now?

Please Can I Have a Man

Please can I have a man who wears corduroy.
Please can I have a man
who knows the names of 100 different roses;
who doesn't mind my absent-minded rabbits
wandering in and out
as if they own the place,
who makes me creamy curries from fresh lemon-grass,
who walks like Belmondo in *A Bout de Souffle*;
who sticks all my carefully-selected postcards –
sent from exotic cities
he doesn't expect to come with me to,
but would if I asked, which I will do –
with nobody else's, up on his bedroom wall,
starting with Ivy, the Famous Diving Pig,
whose picture, in action, I bought ten copies of;
who talks like Belmondo too, with lips as smooth
and tightly-packed as chocolate-coated
(*melting* chocolate) peony buds;
who knows that piling himself stubbornly on top of me
like a duvet stuffed with library books and shopping-bags
is all too easy: please can I have a man
who is not prepared to do that.
Who is not prepared to say I'm 'pretty' either.
Who, when I come trotting in from the bathroom
like a squealing freshly-scrubbed piglet
that likes nothing better than a binge
of being affectionate and undisciplined and uncomplicated,
opens his arms like a trough for me to dive into.

Ted Hughes

Destiny, not guilt, was enough
For Actaeon. It is no crime
To lose your way in a dark wood.

It happened on a mountain where hunters
Had slaughtered so many animals
The slopes were patched red with the butchering places.

When shadows were shortest and the sun's heat hardest
Young Actaeon called a halt:
'We have killed more than enough for the day.

'Our nets are stiff with blood,
Our spears are caked, and our knives
Are clogged in their sheaths with the blood of a glorious hunt.

Let's be up again in the grey dawn –
Back to the game afresh. This noon heat
Has baked the stones too hot for a human foot.'

All concurred. And the hunt was over for the day.
A deep cleft at the bottom of the mountain
Dark with matted pine and spiky cypress

Was known as Gargaphie, sacred to Diana,
Goddess of the hunt.
In the depths of this goyle was the mouth of a cavern

That might have been carved out with deliberate art
From the soft volcanic rock.
It half-hid a broad pool, perpetually shaken

By a waterfall inside the mountain,
Noisy but hidden. Often to that grotto,
Aching and burning from her hunting,

Diana came
To cool the naked beauty she hid from the world.
All her nymphs would attend her.

One held her javelin,
Her quiverful of arrows and her unstrung bow.
Another folded her cape.

Two others took off her sandals, while Crocale
The daughter of Ismenus
Whose hands were the most artful, combing out

The goddess' long hair, that the hunt had tangled,
Bunched it into a thick knot,
Though her own hair stayed as the hunt had scattered it.

Five others, Nephele, Hyale, Phiale
Psecas and Rhanis, filled great jars with water
And sluiced it over Diana's head and shoulders.

The goddess was there, in her secret pool,
Naked and bowed
Under those cascades from the mouths of jars

In the fastness of Gargaphie, when Actaeon,
Making a beeline home from the hunt
Stumbled on this gorge. Surprised to find it,

He pushed into it, apprehensive, but
Steered by a pitiless fate – whose nudgings he felt
Only as surges of curiosity.

So he came to the clearing. And saw ripples
Flocking across the pool out of the cavern.
He edged into the cavern, under ferns

That dripped with spray. He peered
Into the gloom to see the waterfall –
But what he saw were nymphs, their wild faces

Screaming at him in a commotion of water.
And as his eyes adjusted, he saw they were naked,
Beating their breasts as they screamed at him.

And he saw they were crowding together
To hide something from him. He stared harder.
Those nymphs could not conceal Diana's whiteness,

The tallest barely reached her navel. Actaeon
Stared at the goddess, who stared at him.
She twisted her breasts away, showing him her back.

Glaring at him over her shoulder
She blushed like a dawn cloud
In that twilit grotto of winking reflections,

And raged for a weapon – for her arrows
To drive through his body.
No weapon was to hand – only water.

So she scooped up a handful and dashed it
Into his astonished eyes, as she shouted:
'Now, if you can, tell how you saw me naked.'

That was all she said, but as she said it
Out of his forehead burst a rack of antlers.
His neck lengthened, narrowed, and his ears

Folded to whiskery points, his hands were hooves,
His arms long slender legs. His hunter's tunic
Slid from his dappled hide. With all this

The goddess
Poured a shocking stream of panic terror
Through his heart like blood. Actaeon

Bounded out across the cave's pool
In plunging leaps, amazed at his own lightness.
And there

Clear in the bulging mirror of his bow-wave
He glimpsed his antlered head,
And cried: 'What has happened to me?'

No words came. No sound came but a groan.
His only voice was a groan.
Human tears shone on his stag's face

From the grief of a mind that was still human.
He veered first this way, then that.
Should he run away home to the royal palace?

Or hide in the forest? The thought of the first
Dizzied him with shame. The thought of the second
Flurried him with terrors.

But then, as he circled, his own hounds found him.
The first to give tongue were Melampus
And the deep-thinking Ichnobates.

Melampus a Spartan, Ichnobates a Cretan.
The whole pack piled in after.
It was like a squall crossing a forest.

Dorceus, Pamphagus and Oribasus –
Pure Arcadians. Nebrophonus,
Strong as a wild boar, Theras, as fierce.

And Laelaps never far from them. Pterelas
Swiftest in the pack, and Agre
The keenest nose. And Hylaeus

Still lame from the rip of a boar's tusk.
Nape whose mother was a wolf, and Poemenis –
Pure sheep-dog. Harpyia with her grown pups,

Who still would never leave her.
The lanky hound Laden, from Sicyon,
With Tigris, Dromas, Canace, Sticte and Alce,

And Asbolus, all black, and all-white Leuca.
Lacon was there, with shoulders like a lion.
Aello, who could outrun wolves, and Thous,

Lycise, at her best in a tight corner,
Her brother Cyprius, and black Harpalus
With a white star on his forehead.

Lachne, like a shaggy bear-cub. Melaneus
And the Spartan-Cretan crossbreeds
Lebros and Agriodus. Hylactor,

With the high, cracked voice, and a host of others,
Too many to name. The strung-out pack
Locked onto their quarry,

Flowed across the landscape, over crags,
Over cliffs where no man could have followed,
Through places that seemed impossible.

Where Actaeon had so often strained
Every hound to catch and kill the quarry,
Now he strained to shake the same hounds off –

His own hounds. He tried to cry out:
'I am Actaeon – remember your master,'
But his tongue lolled wordless, while the air

Belaboured his ears with hounds' voices.
Suddenly three hounds appeared, ahead,
Raving towards him. They had been last in the pack.

But they had thought it out
And made a short cut over a mountain.
As Actaeon turned, Melanchaetes

The ringleader of this breakaway trio
Grabbed a rear ankle
In the trap of his jaws. Then the others,

Theridamus and Oristrophus, left and right,
Caught a foreleg each, and he fell.
These three pinned their master, as the pack

Poured onto him like an avalanche.
Every hound filled its jaws
Till there was hardly a mouth not gagged and crammed

With hair and muscle. Then began the tugging and the ripping.
Actaeon's groan was neither human
Nor the natural sound of a stag.

Now the hills he had played on so happily
Toyed with the echoes of his death-noises.
His head and antlers reared from the heaving pile.

And swayed – like the signalling arm
Of somebody drowning in surf.
But his friends, who had followed the pack

To this unexpected kill,
Urged them to finish the work. Meanwhile they shouted
For Actaeon – over and over for Actaeon

To hurry and witness this last kill of the day –
And such a magnificent beast –
As if he were absent. He heard his name

And wished he were as far off as they thought him.
He wished he was among them
Not suffering this death but observing

The terrible method
Of his murderers, as they knotted
Muscles and ferocity to dismember

Their own master.
Only when Actaeon's life
Had been torn from his bones, to the last mouthful,

Only then
Did the remorseless anger of Diana,
Goddess of the arrow, find peace.

Jamie McKendrick

ANCIENT HISTORY

The year began with baleful auguries:
comets, eclipses, tremors, forest fires,
the waves lethargic under a coat of pitch
the length of the coastline. And a cow spoke,
which happened last year too, although last year
no one believed cows spoke. Worse was to come.
There was a bloody rain of lumps of meat
which flocks of gulls snatched in mid-air
while what they missed fell to the ground
where it lay for days without festering.
Then a wind tore up a forest of holm-oaks
and jackdaws pecked the eyes from sheep.
Officials construing the Sibylline books
told of helmeted aliens occupying
the crossroads, and high places of the city.
Blood might be shed. Avoid, they warned,
factions and in-fights. The tribunes claimed
this was the usual con-trick
trumped up to stonewall the new law
about to be passed. Violence was only curbed
by belief in a rumour that the tribes
to the east had joined forces and forged
weapons deadlier than the world has seen
and that even then the hooves of their scouts
had been heard in the southern hills.
The year ended fraught with the fear of war.
Next year began with baleful auguries.

BONESHAKER

'"Is it about a bicycle", he asked.' – Flann O'Brien

My not having read *The Third Policeman*
left the piece I'd meant to write on bicycles
seriously under-researched, to put it politely,

as you did, but even before that crucial omission
the whole idea was a non-starter given
I'd never recollect with anything like

tranquillity the strong emotion I experienced
when some sly thief under cloak of darkness
coaxed my racer from the plastic drainpipe

I'd chained it to. No matter that it cost a fiver
from a Hackney scrapyard whose curator
sat throned on an armchair which long ago

may have looked less like a padded dishrag.
Feed the cats, he growled at his thin crony
who began to saw in half an industrial can

of whalemeat while their nine cats, nine lives apiece,
that's as many as eighty-one lives, converged on him
like a raddled orchestra of shofars.

I saw the bike at once and lifted it sky-high
with the distal phalanx of my little finger.
It was as light as a bird not as a feather

like Valéry suggested the true poem should be.
Its lightness was such that it must have been stolen
even then, or especially then, but I eyed it

as Phaeton must have eyed his father's chariot.
I can see you're straight up, the man told my friend
and then (as if aware he'd left me out)

I'm not saying that you're a villain.
But wheels don't come as narrow as those wheels are.
You could pawn that pushbike in a piss-hole.

Eh? Without more words I paid hard cash
but the next day going down the Ball's Pond Road
on that brace of shakes with its shaky brakes

I achieved an unrehearsed forwards roll
across a windscreen the way those Cretan girls
would flip over the horns of a bull, which as

Picasso noted were the shapes of handlebars
but that story's been told. One life later,
the man who'd scythed me down was whistling:

The speed you were going was more like the wind
than the wind itself, an image
he must have known would more than make amends

for the fact that the bike was never quite the same
with a crotchety click at its cotter-pin
and a kerbward-biased front wheel which wore down

one breakblock like a schauchled heel though still
it was fleet as Achilles and a sight less warlike,
being one of mankind's few benign inventions

though the truth is I can't help but hope
it's been far from benign to the one who stole it.
May he bruise his shins – ouch – on those pedals.

for Bernard O'Donoghue

Andrew Motion

FRESH WATER
In Memory of Ruth Haddon

1

This is a long time ago. I am visiting my brother, who is living
near Cirencester, and he says let's go and see the source of the
Thames.
It's winter. We leave early, before the sun has taken frost off the
fields,

and park in a lane. There's a painful hawthorn hedge with a
stile.
When we jump down, our boots gibber on the hard ground.
Then we're striding, kicking ice-dust off the grass to look
confident –

because really we're not sure if we're allowed to be here.
In fact we're not even sure that this is the right place.
A friend of a friend has told us; it's all as vague as that.

In the centre of the field we find more hawthorn, a single
bush,
and water oozing out of a hole in the ground. I tell my brother
I've read about a statue that stands here, or rather lounges
here –

a naked, shaggy-haired god tilting an urn with one massive
hand.
Where is he? There's only the empty field glittering,
and a few dowager cows picking among the dock-clumps.

Where is Father Thames? My brother thinks he has been
                                        vandalised
and dragged off by the fans of other rivers – they smashed the
                                        old man's urn,
and sprayed his bare chest and legs with the names of rivals:

Trent, Severn, Nene, Humber. There's nothing else to do,
so I paddle through the shallow water surrounding the spring,
treading carefully to keep things in focus,

and stoop over the source as though I find it fascinating.
It is fascinating. A red-brown soft-lipped cleft
with bright green glass right up to the edge,

and the water twisting out like a rope of glass.
It pulses and shivers as it comes, then steadies
into the pool, then roughens again as it drains into the valley.

My brother and I are not twenty yet. We don't know who we
                                        are,
Or who we want to be. We stare at the spring, at each other,
and back at the spring again, saying nothing.

A pheasant is making its blatant *kok-kok*
from the wood running along the valley floor.
I stamp both feet and disappear in a cloud.

2

One March there's suddenly a day as warm as May, and my
                                        friend
uncovers the punt he has bought as a wreck and restored,
cleans her, slides her into the Thames near Lechlade, and sets off

upriver. Will I go with him? No, I can't.
But I'll meet him on the water meadows at the edge of town.
I turn out of the market square, past the church, and down
                                        the yew-tree walk.

Shelley visited here once – it's called Shelley's Walk –
but he was out of his element. Here everything is earth
and water, not fire and air. The ground is sleepy-haired

after winter, red berries and rain matted into it.
Where the yew-tree walk ends I go blind in the sun for a
                                        moment,
then it's all right. There's the river beyond the boggy meadows,

hidden by reed-forests sprouting along its banks. They're
                                        dead,
the reeds – a shambles of broken, broad, pale-brown leaves
and snapped bullrush heads. And there's my friend making

his slow curve towards me. The hills rise behind him
in a gradual wave, so that he seems at the centre of an enormous
amphitheatre. He is an emblem of something;

somebody acting something. The punt pole shoots up
wagging its beard of light, falls, and as he moves ahead
he leans forward, red-faced and concentrating.

He's expert but it's slow work. As I get closer I can hear
water pattering against the prow of the punt,
see him twisting the pole as he plucks it out of the gluey
                                        river-bed.

I call to him and he stands straight, giving a wobbly wave.
We burst into laughter. He looks like a madman, floating
                                        slowly
backwards now that he has stopped poling. I must look

like a madman too, mud-spattered and heavy-footed on the
                                                    bank,
wondering how I'm going to get on board without falling in.
As I push open the curtain of leaves to find a way,

I see the water for the first time, solid-seeming and mercury-
                                                    coloured.
Not like a familiar thing at all. Not looking
as though it could take us anywhere we wanted to go.

   3

I've lived here for a while, and up to now the river has been
for pleasure. This evening people in diving suits have taken it
                                                    over.
Everyone else has been shooshed away into Christchurch
                                                    Meadow

or onto Folly Bridge like me. No one's complaining. The
                                          summer evening
expands lazily, big purple and gold clouds building over the
                                          Cumnor hills.
I have often stood here before. Away to the left you can see
                                          Oxford

throwing its spires into the air, full of the conceited joy of
                                          being itself.
Straight ahead the river runs calmly between boat-houses
before losing patience again, pulling a reed-shawl round its ears,

snapping off willows and holding their scarified heads
                                          underwater.
Now there's a small rowing boat, a kind of coracle below me,
and two policemen with their jackets off. The men shield their
                                          eyes,

peering, and almost rock overboard, they're so surprised,
when bubbles erupt beside them and a diver bobs up –
just his head, streaming in its black wet-suit. There are shouts –

See anything? – but the diver shrugs, and twirls his murky
                                        torchlight
with an invisible hand. Everyone on the bridge stops talking.
We think we are about to be shown the story of the river-bed –

its shopping trolleys and broken boat-parts, its lolling bottles,
its plastic, its dropped keys, its blubbery and bloated corpse.
But nothing happens. The diver taps his mask and disappears,

his fart-trail surging raucously for a moment, then subsiding.
The crowd in Christchurch Meadow starts to break up.
On Folly Bridge people begin talking again, and as someone
                                        steps

off the pavement onto the road, a passing grocery van –
irritated by the press of people, and impatient with whatever
brought them together – gives a long wild *paarp* as it revs
                                        away.

4

Now the children are old enough to see what there is to see
we take them to Tower Bridge and explain how the road lifts up,
how traitors arrived at Traitor's Gate, how this was a brewery

and that was a warehouse, how the river starts many miles
                                        inland
and changes and grows, changes and grows, until it arrives here,
London, where we live, then winds past Canary Wharf

(which they've done in school) and out to sea.
Afterwards we lean on the railings outside a café. It's autumn.
The water is speckled with leaves, and a complicated tangle of
                                                          junk

bumps against the embankment wall: a hank of bright grass,
a rotten bullrush stem, a fragment of dark polished wood.
One of the children asks if people drown in the river, and I
                                                          think

of Ruth, who was on the *Marchioness*. After her death, I met
someone who had survived. He had been in the lavatory when
                                                          the dredger hit,
and fumbled his way out along a flooded corridor, his shoes

and clothes miraculously slipping off him, so that when he at
                                                          last
burst into the air he felt that he was a baby again
and knew nothing, was unable to help himself, aghast.

I touch my wife's arm and the children gather round us.
We are the picture of a family on an outing. I love it. I love the
                                                          river
and the perky tour-boats with their banal chat. I love the snub
                                                          barges.

I love the whole dazzling cross-hatchery of traffic and currents,
shadows and sun, standing still and moving forward.
The tangle of junk bumps the wall below me again and I look
                                                          down.

There is Ruth swimming back upstream, her red velvet party
                                                          dress
flickering round her heels as she twists through the locks
and dreams round the slow curves, slithering on for miles

until she has passed the ponderous diver at Folly Bridge
and the reed-forests at Lechlade, accelerating beneath bridges
and willow branches,
slinking easily among the plastic wrecks and weedy trolleys,

speeding and shrinking and silvering until finally she is sliding
uphill
over bright green grass and into the small wet mouth of the
earth,
where she vanishes.

Susan Wicks

My Father is Shrinking

When we last hugged each other
in the garage,
our two heads were level.
Over his shoulder I could see
potato-sacks.

Another season
and in the dusty sunlight
I shall gather him to me,
smooth his collar,
bend to listen
for his precious breathing.

When he reaches
to my waist,
I shall no longer
detach his small hands
from my skirt,
escape his shrill voice
in the dawn garden.

When he comes to my knees,
I shall pick him up and rock him,
rub my face on the white
stubble of his cheek,
see his silver skull
gleam up at me
through thin combings.

On Re-recording Mozart

When the throb of her voice was cut off, I drove
through streets white with silence: no sound
but my own engine, as if above or beyond
the gear-change a knife glittered, and love

itself were cut out, its high vibrating tongue
docked with a neat flick as the full reel
still turned, clicking, lashing its little tail
at nothing, and silence became her whole song.

Now I have re-recorded Mozart, my tape
unwinding across chasms. Between one note
and the next she still breathes. Her breath

pulls me across darkness, the last escape
of bodies. Rising from her new throat
it redeems and redeems us. I have erased death.

C K Williams

1

All under the supposition that he's helping her because she's so
    often melancholy lately,
he's pointing out certain problems with her character, but he's so
    serious, so vehement,
she realizes he's *attacking* her, to hurt, not help; she doesn't know
    what might be driving him,
but she finds she's thinking through his life for him, the losses,
    the long-forgotten sadnesses,
and though she can't come up with anything to correlate with
    how hatefully he's acting,
she thinks *something* has to be there, so she listens, nods, some-
    times she actually agrees.

2

They're only arguing, but all at once she feels anxiety, and real-
    izes she's afraid of him,
then, wondering whether she should risk expressing it to him,
    she understands she can't,
that the way he is these days he'll turn it back on her, and so she
    keeps it to herself,
then, despite herself, she wonders what their life's become to
    have to hide so much,
then comes a wave of disappointment, with herself, not him, and
    not for that initial fear,
but for some cowardice, some deeper dread that makes her ask,
    why not him?

3

He's very distant, but when she asks him what it is, he insists it's
    nothing, though it's not,
she knows it's not, because he never seems to face her and his
    eyes won't hold on hers;
it makes her feel uncertain, clumsy, then as though she's some-
    how supplicating him:
though she wants nothing more from him than she already has –
    what would he think she'd want? –
when she tries to trust him, to believe his offhanded reassurance,
    she feels that she's pretending,
it's like a game, though very serious, like trying to talk yourself
    out of an imminent illness.

4

If there are sides to take, he'll take the other side, against any-
    thing she says, to anyone:
at first she thinks it's just coincidence; after all, she knows she's
    sometimes wrong,
everyone is sometimes wrong, but with him now all there seem
    to be are sides, she's always wrong;
even when she doesn't know she's arguing, when she doesn't
    care, he finds her wrong,
in herself it seems she's wrong, she feels she should apologize, to
    someone, anyone, to him;
him, him, him; what is it that he wants from her: remorse, con-
    trition, should she just *die*?

5

He's telling her in much too intricate detail about a film he's
    seen: she tries to change the subject,
he won't let her, and she finds she's questioning herself – must
    she be so critical, judgmental? –

then she's struck, from something in his tone, or absent from his
tone, some lack of resonance,
that why he's going on about the movie is because there's noth-
ing else to say to her,
or, worse, that there are things to say but not to her, they're too
intimate to waste on her:
it's *she*, she thinks, who's being measured and found wanting, and
what should she think now?

6

This time her, her story, about something nearly noble she once
did, a friend in trouble,
and she helped, but before she's hardly started he's made clear he
thinks it's all a fantasy,
and she as quickly understands that what he really means is that
her love, her love for him,
should reflexively surpass the way she loved, or claims she loved,
the long-forgotten friend,
and with a shock of sorrow, she knows she can't tell him that,
that the betrayal,
and certainly there is one, isn't his desire to wound, but her
thinking that he shouldn't.

7

She sits in his lap, she's feeling lonely, nothing serious, she just
wants sympathy, company,
then she realizes that though she hasn't said a word, he's sensed
her sadness and is irked,
feels that she's inflicting, as she always does, he seems to think,
her misery on him,

so she tells herself not to be so needy anymore, for now, though, she just wants to leave,

except she can't, she knows that if he suspects he's let her down he'll be more irritated still,

and so she stays, feeling dumb and out of place, and heavy, heavier, like a load of stone.

8

She experiences a pleasurable wave of nostalgia, not for her own past, but for his:

she can sense and taste the volume and the textures of the room he slept in as a child,

until she reminds herself she's never been there, never even seen the place, so, reluctantly,

she thinks reluctantly, she wonders if she might not be too close, too devoted to him,

whether she might actually be trying to become him, then she feels herself resolve, to her surprise,

to disengage from him, and such a sense of tiredness takes her that she almost cries.

9

As usual these days he's angry with her, and because she wants him not to be she kisses him,

but perhaps because he's so surprised, she feels him feel her kiss came from some counter-anger,

then she starts to doubt herself, wondering if she might have meant it as he thinks she did,

as a traitor kiss, a Judas kiss, and if that's true, his anger, both his angers, would be justified:

look, though, how he looks at her, with bemusement, hardly hidden, he knows her so well,

he senses her perplexity, her swell of guilt and doubt: how he cherishes his wrath!

10

Such matters end, there are healings, breakings-free; she tells
  herself they end, but still,
years later, when the call she'd dreaded comes, when he calls,
  asking why she hasn't called,
as though all those years it wasn't her who'd called, then stopped
  calling and began to wait,
then stopped waiting, healed, broke free, so when he innocently
  suggests they get together,
she says absolutely not, but feels uncertain – is she being spiteful?
  small? – and then she knows:
after this he'll cause her no more pain, though no matter how
  she wished it weren't, this is pain.

The Best First Collection Poems

Jane Draycott

ELBOW

> *'women who expose their elbows, even in the*
> *sweltering heat, give their husbands sufficient*
> *reason for a divorce'* – Rabbinical ruling, 1994

I am elbow, husband. I am the cup which glistens
here in the secret ruck of her sleeve,
imprinted with children, the wall of a cave.
I am also any sharp turn or change in direction

in the road. I'm an angle, a bent joint or union
where things come together. Which you husband
used to caress, to cup like a breast in a crowd,
at your mother's. Where two things join.

Out-at-elbow's a hound who is not
a straight mover. In this forbidden zone she sweats
a tiny river, a lovely lacework of salt threads
hidden. It is a weakness in the dog.

I know I am what you'd prefer to keep in the dark.
This unweathered snatch of her skin, schoolgirl thin.
The pulse of her, here where her vein
takes the blood home, the way back to her heart.

At-one's-elbow is in close attendance
just when it's needed, near at hand.
You come at her side on, an elbow wind
steering me, pushing her. Ready for use.

The Prince Rupert's Drop

the rapid cooling of this extraordinary glass drop
leaves it in a state of enormous tension…

It's brilliant. It's a tear you can stand a car
on, the hard eye of a chandelier
ready to break down and cry like a baby, a rare
birth, cooled before its time. It's an ear
of glass accidentally sown in the coldest of water,
that sheer drop, rock solid except for the tail
or neck which will snap like sugar, kick like a mortar
under the surefire touch of your fingernail.

It's the pearl in a will-o'-the-wisp, the lantern asleep
in the ice, the light of St Elmo's fire in your eyes.
It's the roulette burst of a necklace, the snap
of bones in an icicle's finger, the snip of your pliers
at the neck of my heart, the fingertip working the spot
which says 'you are here' until you are suddenly not.

Matthew Francis

A Blind Man in the Forest

Yes, I know we're in the open now.
There's grass underfoot and the wind is
longer. Let's sit down. I liked it, though,
in the trees. It was a good, loud place
with plenty of crackling. Did you see
the deer? There it was, going away.

That's the best thing about coming here:
the scenery doesn't wait to be
looked at. It gets on. Today the air
was full of falling. I couldn't see
the leaves coming, so they touched my face
like that, with the forthright gentleness

of a child's hand borrowing my thigh
to help himself on to a train once.
I can smell autumn. The woods are high
and the sun hovers on my hands, tense.
It's friendly still but not intimate.
Water is mixing it somewhere. Let's sit

on these flowers you say are like stars,
very small ones, in the close-cropped grass.
Softer than the stars one remembers,
less prickly. Touchable, though. I miss
distant things. Stars are just an idea.
I live at arms' length. I feel my way

to where I am. I don't even see
darkness. I have nothing to look through.
So I let the forest come to me,
like that deer, and go when it wants to.
Without walls it's an enormous place,
oneself. It's as big . . . as big as this.

Poem Without Words

An afternoon in early you know
it has birds in it the time of year
they're always writing about things grow
the whatever shines. I'm sitting here
trying to read on the patio
and the thing I mentioned earlier
is on the chimney the flying thing
you notice them about now whistling.

They say it never does the same song
twice or is it that no two ones do
the same one as each other? They sing
in their own languages so they know
which is which. It almost means something.
Evening is coming. Before I go
inside I want to finish this – what
the breeze is reading with me. It's shut.

Where have I got to? They're all the same
these these. It was the Swiss artist friend
did it if there was one. No not him
the woman with the pearls and they found
a pearl in the man's suit in the hem
of his hm. Perhaps I'll read the end.
Perhaps I have. I don't want to know
who did it. Who did they do it to?

And now my black visitor is here
rubbing her pointy face against me
like a boy-whatsit starting a fire.
What do you want then? She doesn't say
the one vowel she knows. Do you want your
stuff that comes in a tin? Actually
she'd rather get her hooks into that
small flies it likes to sing you know it

is flexing the usual turns of phrase
on the rooftop but with a new twist.
Today is going inside. Small flies
are stuttering in what is the last
and most elusive light. There it is
again. You know when I heard it first
I must have been oh. Too dark to read
now. It makes you think. Blackbird, blackbird.

Tracey Herd

INDIAN SUMMER

That summer was hotter than any other
in my life-time. My bare knees
itched and burned in the sand
as I dug and dug for the rusted coins
that Nanny had hidden that morning.
I'd watched her from my bedroom window.

The rugs hung heavy on the line
with a row of scalps put there to dry –
my whole family wiped out by Indians,
shock woven brightly into their faces.

The sky burned blue as a flame.
Grass browned. I could have rubbed
two stones together and the flare
would have shot me like a rocket
into the wilderness.

I exchanged the coins for a pony
the colour of gun-metal
and hoisted myself up into the saddle,
wincing as my half-peeled thighs
stuck to the hot leather,
and punctured his flanks with my spurs.
He hollered, balancing on his shaggy hind legs
before hitting the dirt at a gallop.

He stretched out over the blazing pampas
leaving my mother lying awkwardly
in the gaudily striped deck-chair,
blood dripping delicately
down the cut stem of her neck.

THE SIEGE

The twilight is a cathedral: a hymn
to summer thumps against the rafters
of the sky. The voices of the congregation
are cold and clear as holy water.

The heart is a walled city, thriving
but assailable. Only I know my way
here, each street's history, naming
them for kings and queens. Cramped alleys

bear the names of saints, and the tapestries
hanging in the fine museum
show soldiers under a smoking sky,
heretics dragged from secret rooms.

Their souls were purged and returned to God.
This is another century: my heart is peaceful.
I have unpicked the scarlet and gold threads
of their agony. Their blistered hands embroider angels.

Roddy Lumsden

Fin

The evidence was minimal: no stains,
no trail of blood, just three satsuma skins,
one dressing-gown, in turquoise towelling,

thrown casually on the sofa arm,
and screwed up in the pocket, one page torn
from a diary – in small, neat script, the following:

8.30 – jog with Fanny Blankers-Koen.
9.45 – play chess with Capablanca.
10.30 – dancing lesson, Fred Astaire.

12 noon – deliver theorem to Fermi.
12.45 – send fax to Mao Tse Tung.
1.30 – sit for Lucian …and so on.

Sergeant MacGrillen chewed his pencil stub
and turned to me, 'That thing through in the tub?
It might just be the body of the century.

Might take some time to suss what happened here.'
I shrugged and settled in an easy chair
and lit the last smoke in my pack of twenty.

Yeah Yeah Yeah

No matter what you did to her, she said,
There's times, she said, she misses you, your face
Will pucker in her dream, and times the bed's
Too big. Stray hairs will surface in a place
You used to leave your shoes. A certain phrase,
Some old song on the radio, a joke
You had to be there for, she said, some days
It really gets to her; the way you smoked
Or held a cup, or her, and how you woke
Up crying in the night sometimes, the way
She'd stroke and hush you back, and how you broke
Her still. All this she told me yesterday,
Then she rolled over, laughed, began to do
To me what she so rarely did with you.

Robin Robertson

ARTICHOKE

The nubbed leaves
come away
in a tease of green, thinning
down to the membrane:
the quick, purpled,
beginnings of the male.

Then the slow hairs of the heart:
the choke that guards its trophy,
its vegetable goblet.
The meat of it lies, displayed,
up-ended, *al dente*,
the stub-root aching in its oil.

ESCAPOLOGY

A shallow cut lets the blood bead:
and you could charm red bracelets,
coax necklaces from nowhere.
You stashed blades like savings,
pulled them out with a flourish
in a fan of silver.

Soon it was ribbons from the wrist
and sawing yourself in two; always
trying to disappear.
Then the finale: sedatives, restraints,
the escape-proof box. And you
lying there. A locked knife.

The Best Individual Poems

Harry Clifton

*'I would like to be God in France, where no one believes
anymore. No calls on me, I could sit all day in cafés…'*

> *– Saul Bellow*

Allah of Islam! Yahweh of the Jews!
   They were calling upon me
All over Paris. Sabbaths, but the Bon Dieu
Had gone missing. I had set myself free
From Friday at the mosque, that pile of shoes,
Those thousands praying, Saturday Torah scrolls
And lit menorahs, Sundays salvaging souls –
From Daubenton, Des Rosiers, Saint Gervais,
To live again in the body, *l'homme moyen sensuel*

Adrift on the everyday. Streetlife, glass cafés
   Were my chosen ground.
Whatever I needed easily could be found
In a few square miles. Massage, phlebotomy,
Thalassal brines and hydrotherapeutics,
Mont Sainte Genevieve, with its hermeneutics,
Clichy for hardcore, all the highs and lows
Of pure *bien-être*, like a bird in the hand.
Oh yes, if I wanted a woman, I knew where to go –

And who could deny me? Human, all my horizons
   Were reachable by train
From Austerlitz, Saint Lazare, the Gare de Lyon –
Not that I needed them. Gifted, like Urizen,
With omnipresence, simultaneity,
I could sit here over dinner, and still see
Normandy's apple-belt, or the lightwaves of the South
Collapsing on beaches. None could deny me
The springtime glitter of shad in the rivermouth

Of the long Garonne – that exquisite flesh,
   The bone that sticks in the throats
Of twenty centuries. Ichthyus the fish,
Like Renan's Christ, was dying, dying out
In the boredom of villages, of Proustian spires,
Provincial time, the echo-sounding fleets
Off La Rochelle, the sleep of the Loire,
The happiness that is almost too complete,
The Sunday afternoons that run on Michelin tyres.

Was that terrible? Tell me, was that sad?
   The night of the gods,
Of absences, abscondings, abdications?
Was I to kneel before him, the tramp at the station,
Unpeel his stinking trainers, wash his feet,
Amaze the wage-slaves? In the name of what
Would I drive the midnight circle of philosophers
Out of their TV studios, swivel chairs,
With hempen fire, the rope of castigation?

No, instead I would sit here, I would wait –
   A dinner, a *café crème*,
A chaser of grog. Whatever else, there was time –
Let Judgement take care of itself. To celebrate –
That was the one imperative. Randomness, flux,
Drew themselves about me as I ate,
Protected by the nearnesses of women, their sex
Blown sheer through summer dresses, loving my food,
My freedom, as they say a man should.

Lavinia Greenlaw

A World Where News Travelled Slowly

It could take from Monday to Thursday
and three horses. The ink was unstable,
the characters cramped, the paper tore where it creased.
Stained with the leather and sweat of its journey,
the envelope absorbed each climatic shift,
as well as the salt and grease of the rider
who handed it over with a four-day chance
that by now things were different and while the head
had to listen, the heart could wait.

Semaphore was invented at a time of revolution;
the judgement of swing in a vertical arm. News travelled
letter by letter, along a chain of towers, each built
within telescopic distance of the next.
The clattering mechanics of the six-shutter telegraph
still took three men with all their variables
added to those of light and weather,
to read, record and pass the message on.

Now words are faster, smaller, harder
… *we're almost talking in one another's arms.*
Coded and squeezed, what chance has my voice
to reach your voice unaltered and then to leave no trace?
Nets tighten across the sky and the sea bed. When London
made contact with New York, there were such fireworks
City Hall caught light. It could have burned to the ground.

David Harsent

THE MAKERS

It was pride and nothing else made me lift my head from the spit
and sawdust of The Prospect of Oblivion,
on my cheek
a dark naevus that married

a knobby knot in the planking. How long I'd been down
and out was anybody's guess; I'd guess
an hour or more by the state of my suit,
a foul rag-bag,

by the state of my hair, a patty-cake
of my own ripe keck,
unless it was the keck of Sandy Traill
or Blind Harry, my friends in drink that night,

that aye night, every night, in fact, that I found myself
making the first full dip
into the cream-and-midnight black
of a glass of stout, with a double shot on the side,

the very combination that left me wrecked,
face down, and holding fast to the spar
of a table leg as the room went by, or else
the floor was a wheel . . . The brilliant double zero

of the Prospect's neon logogram swam up
from a two-quart pool of special brew, and I looked
deep for any chance reflection
of Sandy's turnip head, his docile grin, I looked

in hope of a glimpse of Harry's silver-backed
pennyweight dark glasses, taken off, sometimes, with such
graceful delicacy that Harry seemed
to be setting aside a near impossible burden, taken off

to give you the benefit
of a bald faced stare from a couple of weepers white
as the little scalp from a soft-boiled egg, but when
I got to my knees, to my hands and knees, to my feet,

it was just me and the barman, whose face I'd seen
before in another place, but this time kinder and wiser
as he drew me off
one on the house 'to stiffen your backbone',

he said, 'to loosen your joints', which put me in mind
of Sandy going down to a Scotch handshake
followed fast by a boot heel laid
to his kidneys, one of those luminous nights

when you say the wrong thing to the right
person, 'Or perhaps the other way round,' Sandy wondered
as I held a staunch to his face in the closet bathroom
of what he liked to call his 'atelier'

with its bright blue Pompidou pipes, with its half-glass roof,
with a full moon, that night, in a clear sky, and Sandy bearing a
        pint
of blood, at least,
crusted to his shirtfront, and Blind Harry

tapping round in a stark flash-flood
of moonlight, until the ferrule of his cane
knocked the neck of a bottle of Famous Grouse. Remembering
        that,
I remembered a day spent walking the towpath

from Hammersmith down to Kew, a bottle going between us –
this would have been the day
of Francis Bacon dying in Madrid, if not
the day after for sure – and Sandy toppling back

through a common or garden fig as we passed the Pagoda
the bottle upraised, his complaint: 'The dearth of great painters.'
That was a night when none of us went home
to our beds, a night of trial and true confession

as Harry lashed out at himself,
a long, torn, *basso profondo*, sick at heart,
counting off the betrayals, the betrayed, the white nights
returning in wastefulness, the pledges, the pacts,

the business of going cold turkey, the equally tricky
business of turning a blind eye, turning a blind
corner only to find yourself
standing where you stood but ten years older . . .

This was right through the dead hour of the night.
Much later, Harry said: 'In the days when I had my sight,
all I ever feared
was what might tap my shoulder in the dark.'

Thinking back to this, one foot in the neon slop,
the other hoiked on the bar-rail,
it came to me in a rush, along with my third or fourth
pick-me-up, that what Sandy had said that day

was not 'dearth' but 'death',
a thought I chased to the mirror behind the bar
and there he was, the Old Man, larger than life, his eye
like raptor's, raw and quick, who took

Bacon that day in Spain, who took Soutine
and Schiele and Rouault, three who knocked me flat
before I could think, before I knew a thing,
leaving me no way back,

and took John Keats in a room by the Spanish Steps,
stanza della morte, where I caught
one glimpse of the flowered beams and fainted fast,
and took Pierre Bonnard

who delved with me deep in the mysteries
of domesticity, year in, year out, leaving me no way back,
and took the Tam Lin poet, took
the poet of 'Jellon Grame', and took my friend

'Henri de Beaufort', self-styled,
who introduced me first to Jeanne Duval, leaving me no way
        back,
while Baudelaire brayed from his deathbed
– *merde merde merde* – and took

Kirsten Flagstad who delivered up
Kindertotenlieder, a gift outright, the radio on
as I leant from my bedroom window to smoke that night,
that aye night of sleet

and little light and a frozen sea,
brass-bollock weather as Sandy would no doubt have it,
when even on pain of death
I couldn't have told you who in hell was Mahler

or Rückert, and took
Alberto Giacometti, who said, 'The more
I take away the bigger it gets,' thereby
explaining a lot and leaving me no way back, and took

the distant greats like dominoes, *not dearth*
but death, and took Serina Stocker,
who taught me how to flay a hare ('You get
the knife under her scut – see there? – then up

over the paunch, enough to peel and pull,
and it's off like a Babygro'), and took, within a week,
George Stocker who said to all,
'I shall turn my face to the wall, and there's an end,'

and took Giacomo Puccini, who sent me
crying from the hall, too green and feverish
to be clever, and took, one day, a mere face in the crowd,
who fell or stepped

onto the rail, and was brought back up
broken, wide-eyed, a fallen angel, and passed,
like our best ambitions,
from soiled hand to soiled hand,

and took Albert Camus
who dressed me in black and told me to grow a beard
and pronounced me *an Existentialist* through tears
of laughter, and took Sigmund Freud

who sat at my shoulder throughout one bookblind summer
foxing me utterly, and took,
one by one, like a circle closing a circle,
people I should have loved

but wouldn't, leaving me no way back, and took
Walt Whitman and Raymond Chandler and Laurence Sterne,
who hitch-hiked with me
through France and Italy and down to Greece,

the four of us with our toes at the utter brink
of a strip of dual carriageway a mile
beyond the city limits, backed by cornfields,
and darkness coming on with a mist of drizzle,

took them as he's bound to take
whoever might catch his eye, and there's an end
that even the brightest must come to, even the best,
as with the wynd wavis the wickir, even the great

and good, 'even your good
self and my good self', the barman said, putting a cloth
to the mirror where now only a tarnish lay,
nickel and muffled yellow, just below the glass, an end

even for Sandy and Harry, two faces
I'd hoped to see again, but he pulled me 'one for the road'
          and next
I was through the door, the last swallow
still caught in my throat, and walking the precipice

of a four-lane freeway, hearing Whitman's line again
in the beat of an engine
half a mile back, hearing Sandy say,
'There comes a moment when you lay your brush to the canvas

and everything's *ease*, everything's *gift*,
so that even the time it takes
to load your palette is unendurable boredom,' whereupon
Harry turned his head, as if to darkness.

This was just before dawn and the whisky gone.
Much later, I came to see
what Harry might have meant by that sudden
turn-and-shudder, not least as I shuddered in turn,

tenant of that stinking suit, not least
as I bowed my head to a brisk downpour, not least
as the road unravelled
behind me, leaving me no way back, not least

as I considered those days of dog
eat dog ('just blanks' in Sandy's view, 'just blanks', by which
      he meant
canvas, or *pages*), the yards of unread books,
the music stalled on 'pause'

in a room that no one uses any more, my face in the glass
of *Femme debout dans so baignoire*, the sea rising
off the sea wall with a cold, mechanical hiss, the days dug-in
when even the clear

prospect of money couldn't raise the dead-
weight of a way of life gone out of fashion,
days of certain folly, certain fools, a certain
landmark standing out of a day-long mist, the interest

you pay hand over fist, a certain way
of simply getting down the street, a sense
of things going under, a sense of things running to waste,
the knack of living always against the grain, the stinging glare,
      that day,

of the city in negative (just blanks),
as my plane tilted and dropped and I saw the sun
on a stretch of water, nickel and curd yellow, like a stain
under glass, a stain

under the fingernail, not least as I turned that night,
that aye night, and cocked my thumb at a slow-lane juggernaut
decked out with coloured lights like a carousel
and rolling up through the rain.

Craig Raine

RASHOMON: THE OPERA

The Bandit Tajomaru

We had a chance encounter on the Yamashina Road,
His wife was seated sideways on the horse.

He held the bridle in his sunburnt hand and walked,
Her veil was lifted briefly by the breeze.

I saw her face and fell in love.
She had a mole beside her mouth,

a drop of Indian ink still wet.
I could have killed the husband there and then.

Saké at blood temperature, or blood itself –
to someone like me it's all the same.
I've been a bandit all my life.
I have my thirsts to quench.

But somehow I decided otherwise this day.
Perhaps because the Yamashina road can be a busy road.

I told the husband there was treasure in the grove.
A buried hoard of bullion, beryl, lapis lazuli.

The Samurai believed my tale of treasure trove.
She waited with the horse while we forced through the cane.

I overpowered him and tied him up,
The cords cut into his kimono.

He was trussed up like a caterpillar writhing.
The gag was tight and made him look a toothless crone.

I told her that he was taken sick
and led her gently by the hand into the grove.

The bamboo squeezed itself against her flesh
as if the place itself were passionate.

Her hat came off. Her hair came down.
The place was plucking at her clothes.

When she saw her husband bound,
her hand slid out of mine and drew a dagger.

She was angry. I was amused but agile.
Struck, the dagger went out like a light.

I worked my knee between her legs.
Shantung. Hirsute. Digging, digging deep,

I worked the seam. but when I came to go,
she begged, her hair across her mouth,

that one of us should die. I or her husband.
So that her name should not be known to both.

Whoever won the fight would take her for his wife.
The husband rubbed his untied arms.

Our swords unsheathed like shantung silk when torn
and after seven strokes the Samurai was dead,

his last long moan a sigh of satisfaction.
But when I turned the girl had gone.

Her hand in mine was very small.
I ask this court the supreme penalty.

The Wife Masago

I was only nineteen years old, O holy father.
We had been married seven happy months.

When he had used me for his lust and left,
his open blue kimono billowing behind,

I turned to where my husband was tied up.
The gag pulled down the corners of his mouth

So that his face was tragic, a Kabuki mask.
I did not recognise his stranger's eyes.

I searched for tears trembling there
to match the mirage in my own

which made the bamboo curtain faint.
And grow upright again. And faint.

Seeing the hatred in my husband's eyes,
I rearranged my robe to cover this dishonoured flesh.

I said with broken, mended, broken voice:
Takejiro, husband, we cannot live like this.

You saw my shame. And now your nostrils smell my shame.
I am defiled forever and so we both must die.

I will kill you first and then myself,
The expression in my husband's eyes agreed.

Then I saw my dagger shining like the evening star,
uncertain, tearful, on the grass, a million miles away.

I think I said: Takejiro, give me your life.
And I pushed the blade quite easily

like cream cheese left to harden overnight outside.
I must have fainted. I woke up on the forest floor,

old cedar needles like cinnamon next to my eyes.
Takejiro had gone to kiss his ancestors on both cheeks.

But then I couldn't kill myself
because the life in me was strong, too strong to die.

I stabbed my throat and lived.
I threw myself into a lake.

but I felt my body fight for breath on shore.
I hanged myself and was rescued by my hands.

I am only nineteen, father, holy father.
It will take a life to die of shame.

The Husband Takejiro through a Medium

Masago with a mole beside her mouth,
brown, the shiny sepia of an apple seed.

When he had finished with her flesh,
he held her hand and whispered words of comfort.

I wanted to cry across the grove:
do not believe this bandit, love.

He said: your husband will hate you now.
He said: leave your husband, marry me.

Her fingers played among the cedar needles.
He traced the lines of life and love and fate

as if her other hand belonged to him.
His finger waked the paths across her palm.

And then my wife, Masago, agreed to go with him.
We had been married only seven months.

I watched the mole move by her mouth
as my Masago said: But you must kill him now.

I cannot be your wife while he still lives.
He stood up, transfixed, then struck her down.

He came bowlegged across the grove.
His cock in its ruff of hair

was exactly at the level of my eyes.
He said: shall I kill her, or shall I let her live?

For these words I plead that he be pardoned.
I hesitated. Masago with that mole.

I hesitated and she fled beyond his reach.
He took my sword, my bow and arrows,

cut one cord and left without another word.
As I untied my other bonds, I heard someone weeping.

Gradually, this weeping came closer, closer,
until I realised that it was I.

I took Masago's dagger from the forest floor,
wiped it clean and stabbed myself.

I was there forever while the darkness came.
Night came like a woman's hair over my face.

The stars shone up above like dagger points.
The blood was cold and hard as frozen snow.

At dawn someone I could not see crept in the grove
and drew the dagger out and blood was bitter in my mouth.

The Woodcutter

Your honour, I was chopping wood.
My right hand slid from head to haft.

Sweet cedar chips were spurting in the gloom like sparks.
The Yamashina Road was five hundred yards away.

The head of the axe worked loose.
I stopped and stooped to wedge it tight.

And then I heard a harness creak.
I heard the clink of bit.

I heard the horse's breath.
But bamboo canes came thick between.

I could not see. I saw the aftermath.
A grove of trampled grass

and a body in a blue kimono.
Dead from a single sword wound in the chest.

A bluebottle was walking in the thin-lipped wound.
Shantung. Hirsute. Beryl. Lapis lazuli.

There was a coil of cord.
Can I leave the court, your excellency?

I am a poor peasant, lord.
Firs are waiting to be felled.

Ensemble: Bandit, Wife, Husband, Woodcutter

I killed her husband with my father's sword.
The seventh stroke.

Where his kimono parted when he took a breath,
there I pushed the dagger slowly in.

I took the dagger she had dropped
and drove it into my dishonoured heart.

I untied the husband's bonds and beat him in fair fight.
He fell, both hands bleeding where he held the sword.

His look of loathing was a clear demand for death.
Give me your life and I will follow like a shadow at your heels.

I tried to sacrifice myself so many different ways.
But bodies are not brutes you drive into the abattoir.

I wished to ride her as a rider rides a horse
in battle. Selfishly. Unthinking. Harsh.

I was chopping wood.
No. My right hand slid from head to haft.

Sweat cedar chips like sparks.
No. My seed was spurting in the gloom like sparks.

I was really after buried treasure.
I was after complicated pleasure:

to violate the girl before her spouse,
this way, that way, in front, behind, without a pause.

Soon the other's breath will fight for breath,
the reek of rope around his neck.

Between his legs a heavy saddle
and an upward curving pommel.

It was the mole beside her mouth.
It made me realise that love is not a myth.

He rode his mount into the ground,
till she was broken, saddled, reined.

My heart was ripped like shantung silk.
I felt each fibre break

and slowly tear the tear across.
Whatever happened happened to the missing horse.

The heart of darkness tolling, tolling.
Seven strokes and stopped.

Cold air of evening and fingers feeling for the dagger
when they find my soul and fling it far from me.

Carol Rumens

A Day in the Life of Farmer Dream

In the morning light I stand outside my limits,
With equanimity survey the fields,
The thorn-hemmed acres that I call my land.
Some are ploughed, some newly sown, some thick
Already with astonishing wheat: some wait
Under a tat of kelp, or bask in clover.
In the morning light I lightly weigh my tasks:
A strong-jawed tractor stands on the hill-top,
†the day burns to be off, time is enormous.
What happens in between I couldn't say –
But the grass has grown, and I return on foot,
A tinker or a tourist, one who gambled,
Perhaps, or dawdled over skip and scrapyard,
Or slept because the blue was cradle-curved,
And ownership, a gleam under a shawl.
Back west, the lying day projects its harvest
Of goldshine; dew is deepening round each stone,
And mist and I will climb the hill, soon, seeking
A house that wears the plume of our dissolving.

The Other Poems

John Agard

MILLENNIUM BUG

The bug threatens a domino-effect global collapse of computer systems at midnight on 31 December 1999. Designed in the sixties with a two-digit number representing the day, month and year, computers are unable to recognise a change of century which requires four digits. Thus at the turn of the year 2000, the new century will be 00, which computers will understand as 1900. And the fear is it could lead to a Mad Max-type Armageddon.
David Atkinson
The Big Issue, 20-26 May 1996

What do they expect when they heed not
    the dance of numbers?

Blunders and bloomers
    will be their undoing

bugs will flower in their computers
    for it is written a day will come

when the angel of mayhem
    appears in their IT systems

and demons disguised as digits
    trumpet the collapse of world markets

that trespass on the human soul
    and treat people as dispensable

and the millennium will toll
    its software Armageddon .

and zero will be lifted high
    as the laughter of Galileo

and Pythagoras too will erupt
   at the mention of bankrupt

and the Devil alone
   shall sing in praise

   of the counting frame
     and runic rods
     and notched bone

Gillian Allnutt

THE GARDEN IN ESH WINNING

Go then into the unfabricated dark
With your four bare crooked tines, fork,
And get my grandmother out of that muddle of dock and
        dandelion root
And put an end to neglect
While the wind says only *Esh Esh*
In the late apple blossom, in the ash
And all the hills rush down to Durham
Where the petulant prince bishops dream
In purple vaults.
It's not the earth's fault,
Fork, but mine, that I for forty years of days and nights invented
        dragons
To guard my grandmother's bare arthritic bones
From my own finding. Now of all things I imagine a garden
Laid over, and dumb as, a disused coalmine.
In the north there are no salley gardens, no, nor bits of willow
        pattern
Plate to plead for me, no, only bones
Unmourned, the memory of the memory of a plane shot down
And its discolouration.
Who now humbly brings me my grandmother in pieces
Like Osiris,
Fork? Who eases out old sorrel gone to seed, old scallions?
Who pulls the purple columbines
Out of the not quite dark midsummer midnight? In the north
        the sky is green,
The long grass, partly shorn, lies down like a lion
And *something's happened to John*
And in this valley of discoloured bones

Ezekiel lies open to the wind, the fork-work done.
The Bible propped like an elbow on the ironing-board within
The house is full of visions, Gran,
Of what we are, were, always might have been.

My grandmother's son John was an RAF navigator, shot down
over France in 1943. The night it happened, she woke and sat up in bed
saying 'Something's happened to John'.

Moniza Alvi

The Job

You have thrown the job to the stars,
but they return it despairingly.
They do not want it either.

You observe it jumping over the moon
more energetic than the cow.
It soars upwards – an ungainly creature

carrying on its back a freight
of appraisal documents and schedules.
It flies without you,

without your eyebrows,
your insight,
your frenzied anticipation,

your briefcase of improbabilities.
Wherever it lands
it will arrive on the dot,

or an hour or two earlier.
Open the post. Begin the day.

A R Ammons

How Things Go Wrong

One person short-cuts across the lawn because
a new building is being added to the complex,
changing everything,

and his shoes press the grass over so
another walker sees a way already waged, and
pretty soon the root texture, like linen,

loosens on the ground, worn through: rain
puddles in a heelprint so walkers walk
around, broadening direction's swath: more

rain widens the mud so that given the picky waywardness
of walkers one could soon drive a chariot
right down the middle of recent developments.

Simon Armitage

THE TYRE

Just how it came to rest where it rested,
miles out, miles from the last farmhouse even,
was a fair question. Dropped by hurricane
or aeroplane perhaps for some reason,
put down as a cairn or marker, then lost.
Tractor-size, six or seven feet across,
it was sloughed, unconscious, warm to the touch,
its gashed, rhinoceros, sea-lion skin
nursing a gallon of rain in its gut.
Lashed to the planet with grasses and roots,
it had to be cut. Stood up it was drunk
or slugged, wanted nothing more than to slump,
to spiral back to its circle of sleep,
dream another year in its nest of peat.
We bullied it over the moor, drove it,
pushed from the back or turned it from the side,
unspooling a thread in the shape and form
of its tread, in its length and in its line,
rolled its weight through broken walls, felt the shock
when it met with stones, guided its sleepwalk
down to meadows, fields, onto level ground.
There and then we were one connected thing,
five of us, all hands steering a tall ship
or one hand fingering a coin or ring.

Once on the road it picked up pace, free-wheeled,
then moved up through the gears, and wouldn't give
to shoulder-charges, kicks; resisted force
until to tangle with it would have been
to test bone against engine or machine,
to be dragged in, broken, thrown out again
minus a limb. So we let the thing go,
leaning into the bends and corners

balanced and centred, riding the camber,
carried away with its own momentum.
We pictured an incident up ahead:
life carved open, gardens in half, parted,
a man on a motorbike taken down,
a phone-box upended, children erased,
police and an ambulance in attendance,
scuff-marks and the smell of burning rubber,
the tyre itself embedded in a house
or lying in the gutter, playing dead.
But down in the village the tyre was gone,
and not just gone but unseen and unheard of,
not curled like a cat in the graveyard, not
cornered in the playground like a reptile,
or found and kept like a giant fossil.
Not there or anywhere. No trace. Thin air.

Being more in tune with the feel of things
than science and facts, we knew that the tyre
had travelled too fast for its size and mass,
and broken through some barrier of speed,
outrun the act of being driven, steered,
and at that moment gone beyond itself
towards some other sphere, and disappeared.

Phil Bowen

WHAT A LITTLE SCARECROW CAN DO

The scarecrow felt he had a poet in him.
The poet felt he had an apostrophe in him.
An apostrophe that wanted a page.
A page that wanted a bride.
A bride that needed a husband.
A husband who wanted a housewife.
The housewife who wanted a lover.
A lover who wanted to feel safe.
The safe that wanted the money.
The money that made a speech.
The speech that needed an actor.
An actor who needed the part.
The part that needed the whole.
The whole that wasn't enough.
Enough that wasn't enormous.
An enormous waste of talent.
Talent that lost the contest.
The contest that had its own rules.
Rules that were taught in the school.
The school with only one teacher.
A teacher who speaks at his pupils.
His pupils in need of a view.
A view of trees and fields.
Trees and fields and animals.
Animals who lived on a farm.
The farm with the special farmer
who gave all his animals names.
And some of the names rhymed.
Some of the rhymes chimed.

And some of the sun shined
on the children who climbed
(behind) the stile:
And   down   the footpath
the poetry smiled.
The poetry that felt it had a scarecrow in it.

John Burnside

PENITENCE

I was driving into the wind
on a northern road,
the redwoods swaying around me like a black
ocean.
       I'd drifted off: I didn't see the deer
till it bounced away,
the back legs swinging outwards as I braked
and swerved into the tinder
of the verge.
       Soon as I stopped
the headlamps filled with moths
and something beyond the trees was tuning in,
a hard attention
boring through my flesh
to stroke the bone.
       That shudder took so long
to end, I thought the animal had slipped
beneath the wheels, and lay there
quivering.
       I left the engine running; stepped outside;
away, at the edge of the light, a body
shifted amongst the leaves
and I wanted to go, to help, to make it well,
but every step I took
pushed it away.
       Or – no; that's not the truth,
or all the truth:
now I admit my own fear held me back,
not fear of the dark, or that presence
bending the trees;
not even fear, exactly, but the dread
of touching, of colliding with that pain.
I stood there, in the river of the wind,

for minutes; then I walked back to the car
and drove away.
                        I want to think that deer
survived; or, if it died,
it slipped into the blackness unawares.
But now and then I drive out to the woods
and park the car: the headlamps fill with moths;
the woods tune in; I listen to the night
and hear an echo, fading through the trees,
my own flesh in the body of the deer
still resonant, remembered through the fender.

Stephen Dobyns

Cold Marble

These poppies with their heavy heads,
how fragile is their beauty. The wind
knocks them casually to the ground,
a single hard rain will break them.

The weight of their petals, the elements
which attract us, also cause their ruin.
I think of beautiful women I have known,
how few had the strength for their beauty,

how it became a burden, something which
entered the room before they themselves
seemed to enter, meaning it was always
put first, seeiled to exclude them, even

betray them, like finding one's best friend
in the arms of an enemy. Or that whore leaning
against a wall in a parking lot in New York,
a face like a Bellini madonna: she catches

my eye. Want it, she says, do you want it?
As if her beauty were the stranger with whom
she was forced to live. Another woman
who slashed her face, the one who drank,

a third woman who covered her blond hair
with ugly scarves – they hated being second,
of arriving on stage after their beauty,
after the buying and selling was done.

One would think the poppy's beauty
would be its blessing as it is for us,
but for the beautiful how often they hate
how their beauty denies them a life,

as if their beauty were a younger sibling
they had to take care of – has it eaten,
is it properly dressed? – until it becomes
the neuter pronoun. Coinage, cold marble –

truly not oneself; rather, the destroyer
of self. How strong must be the ones who bear
their beauty effortlessly and with grace.
Yet this morning after last night's storm,

I find the poppies sprawled in the dirt –
crimson petals, flesh-colored petals,
their black centers hidden – how relaxed
they seem in their destruction, as if glad

to be a memory. In the nursing home,
a woman over ninety gives her wrecked
cheek a friendly pat. Once this face,
she tells me, could break a man's legs.

Helen Dunmore

THE GETHSEMANE GARDEN COMPETITION

Out of moss and twigs, daisies and fallen cherry blossom,
the chipped bit of a handbag mirror, cottonwool lambs,
I made my Gethsemane garden.

I soldered the circuitry of Easter
on a tin tray, getting everything into proportion
I knew better than to dwarf my green hill with daffodils,
or mould the dank mouth of the tomb
too small to fit in a lamb.

My tray was alive and breathing.
There was dawn in that garden,
the surprise of birds.
I could talk myself down
where ducks paddled soft black mud
in the reeds round the pond.

Ruth Fainlight

THE CORSET LADY

How long is it since I noticed one of those discreet corsetry shops on a leafy side street off the main boulevards, small show-window lined with dull-toned grosgrain drapes against which the sole identifying object on display was the plaster figure, half or quarter life-sized, of a female torso topped by a modestly pretty head and face whose demure vacuous gaze evaded every admirer? The surprisingly full and shapely body would be clasped by an elaborate girdle: boned, hooked, bound and strapped – all the skills of corsetiere-proprietor exhibited like a sampler stitched by an 18th century girl as evidence of her skill, and the truncated lower parts veiled by a frill of faded ecru lace. How delightful to have a little lady like that at home, for my very own. Preferably alive.

My mother would laugh indulgently as I elaborated the fantasy. But later, older, arm in arm with some uncertain young suitor, if I stopped entranced before such an illuminated display, I sensed a certain uneasiness, even alarm, to hear this wish expressed.

By the time I came to appreciate their miniature allure, these figures were anachronisms. Their worn appearance testified that no replacements existed. Chips and knocks inflicted while being moved in and out of the window for trappings to be adjusted or changed, revealed dead white (or crumbling, porous, dirty) plaster under the painted surface. Through the slow effects of time and dust, their painted features darkened into curdled plaster heads with antique coiffures and missing noses – like saints in post-Reformation churches – which still survived in occasional hairdressing salons of the outlying suburbs, or the powdered faces of their increasingly short-winded clientele.

Sometimes, between glowing globes of green and purple liquids in shabby pharmacies, I would sight the plaster figure of a man – proportions similar to those of the corset lady, but usually with all limbs and parts intact – garlanded by bandages, trusses, and splints. The two of them seemed to form a pair: a devoted couple maimed and cruelly separated by the exigencies of survival. But I do not recall any urge to reunite then, nor ever wanting to take the little man home with me.

Peter Finch

ALL I NEED IS THREE PLUMS
apologies to William Carlos Williams

I have sold your jewellery collection,
which you kept in a box, forgive me.
I am sorry, but it came upon me
and the money was so inviting, so sweet
and so cold.

I have failed to increase my chest measurements
despite bar bells
and my t-shirt is not full of ripples.
I am sweet but that is no consolation.
You hand is cold.

I did not get the job, your brother did.
He is a bastard I told him, forgive me.
The world is full of wankers, my sweet.

I have lost the dog, I am sorry.
He never liked me, I am hardly inviting.
I took him off the lead in the park and
the swine chased a cat I couldn't
be bothered to run after him.
Forgive me, I will fail less in the
future.

I have collected all the furniture I could find
and dismembered it in the grate, I am sorry,
but I have these aberrations.
The weather is inclement. You have run out of
firelighters.
It's bloody cold.

Please forgive me, I have taken the money
you have been saving in the ceramic pig
and spent it on drink, so sweet and inviting.
This is just to say I am in the pub
where I have purchased the fat guy from
Merthyr's entire collection of scratch and win.
All I need now is three delicious plums.

Forgive me, sweetie,
these things just happen.

Linda France

HER DOGNESS

Life as we knew it has come to an end
since you arrived, puking on our shoulders
in the car. Now, things get done with you

chewing our shoelaces, ankles, the dip
of my best frock, whatever you can get
your teeth into. So who wants to keep

a tidy house when there's the pink of your belly
to be tickled? The speckled thrush
of your muzzle to be nuzzled and stroked?

The irrepressible wag of your white-
tipped tail to lift the corners of my mouth?
All I want is a collie dog to walk with

across the fell, watching the wind
ripple across her back like a dark field
of wheat. Your tongue comes undone like a belt.

My nose is wet. But best is when we come
home and stretch out in front of the fire, two
mad and muddy humbugs who are getting

to know the sound of each other's snores;
two legs and four legs, dreaming of more legs.

W N Herbert

"I grant the wives of Weinsberg
Permission to go forth,
And each may bear the treasure
She deems of highest worth.
Each woman with her burden
Shall find a peaceful way;
A King the word hath spoken –
The King shall none gainsay!"
– David Grant

It was time to get it over with:
all morning the mocking sharpening,
the concerted whetting of steel,
had circled Weinsberg's walls.
Then the east port was finally opened; so
easy a yielding after long months
of this rough wooing, and,
preceded by their shambling priests,
the women all walked out on war.

At first there came
a simultaneous appraisal. So these,
the besiegers thought, were
the promised conquests, scores on scores
of anticipated rapes, now withheld
by their leader's snatch at chivalry.

So this, the women thought,
is the state of our fields, so patiently tilled,
now ripped up by ballista and wheeled tower,
shat upon for months.
At least the earth would be fertile.

And then the bundles on the women's backs
resolved themselves in the gaining light
into emaciated males, the very men
who'd slopped out piss and oil and stones,
spat arrows till the town ran dry of feathers:
those recognised faces. Conrad's officers had
to run down the lines slapping pikestaffs
with their swords. In his tent
the winner laughed, projecting chronicles,
weighing how much massacre his
fledgeling reputation could take.

At last the command came
to let the procession through.
Hosannas rose, and one girl slipped
her heavy brother to the soil. Instantly
the letter of his order was obeyed
and the supine man was spitted.

Then the harrying began, over yards
and miles, as each woman reached
her limit and let her
lover, father, child, touch
their familiar earth. Only a few
troops were needed, to track
this staggering pack,
handle the amount of fight
the menfolk had left in them.
Some women made it a league,
some made it two; some made it to
the ruins of the neighbouring town.

Then there was one woman, in her forties, with
her one late baby, standing at
the roadside shrine, mumbling, till
she could stand no more; she sank,
keeping the boy upon her lap,
so no limb could reach the ground.
When Conrad heard
how he was lame
he let that infant live.

Jane Holland

THEY ARE A TABLEAU AT THE KISSING-GATE

Maids of honour, bridegroom, bride,
the best man in a grey silk suit,
a flash to catch them in the arching
stone, confettied by a sudden gust –
an apple-tree in full white spread
beyond the reach of bone and dust.

I am the driver in a passing car:
the wedding-dress a cloud of lace.
A small hand clutching at a skirt,
some nervous bridesmaid, eight
or maybe nine years old, has seen
the blossom fall, has closed her eyes –

her head falls back into the scent,
the soundless whirr and whirl of earth-
bound petals, like sycamore seeds
on a current of air, silent helicopters
bringing light – a wedding-gift
the bride will brush away, unconsciously.

This is no ordinary act, no summer fête,
another simple wedding held in June.
This is the wind shaking the apple-tree,
the bell above the kissing-gate,
the sudden fall of blossom into light
which only love and innocence can see.

We must be held accountable to love:
where they step out together arm in arm
as newly-weds, spring-cleaned, and climb
into a waiting car beneath a summer sky,
the blossom will still fall, unstoppable –
a drift of change across a changeless time.

Ted Hughes

PLATFORM ONE

Holiday squeals, as if all were scrambling for their lives,
Panting aboard the 'Cornish Riviera'.
Then overflow of relief and luggage and children,
Then ducking to smile out as the station moves.

Out there on the platform, under the rain,
Under his rain-cape, helmet and full pack,
Somebody, head bowed reading something,
Doesn't know he's missing his train.

He's completely buried in that book.
He's forgotten utterly where he is.
He's forgotten Paddington, forgotten
Timetables, forgotten the long, rocking

Cradle of a journey into the golden West,
The coach's soft wingbeat – as light
And straight as a dove's flight.
Like a graveyard statue sentry cast

In blackened old bronze. Is he reading poems?
A letter? The burial service? The raindrops
Beaded along his helmet rim are bronze.
The words on his page are bronze. Their meanings bronze.

Sunk in his bronze world he stands, enchanted.
His bronze mind is deep among the dead.
Sunk so deep among the dead that, much
As he would like to remember us all, he cannot.

Fred Johnston

MUSIC
for Máirtín O Connor

We talk about it in some fashion
every time we meet
the characteristics of the Irish psyche
low-hung weather like muslin over the eyes
a tendency to think too much about ourselves
and what this sun-lack does to poetry

a grainy drift of history
moves over the pier at Annaghdown
Raftery's sung dead under the blowy water
the note wind makes on the lip of a reed
the shape of music working in the bone –
the sacrament of dreaming turned to sound.

Stephen Knight

THE SURF MOTEL

Across the waves that vague, moss-covered knell
Drifting from The Surf Motel
's the dinner bell.

Starfish pack the car park at the height of every swell.

As always, every peal
Calls forth another conger eel
To nibble at the edges of the evening meal.

Silt and seaweed feast upon the carpets they conceal.

All evening, cleaners bail
Black water out of poky rooms to no avail –
Their patience and their buckets fail.

In hoover bags, like escapologists, fish flail

But still,
While tides will ruin everyone they fill,
Visitors remain for weeks, for years perhaps, until; until.

The cost of staying blurs on every bill.

Sarah Maguire

THE INVISIBLE MENDER (MY FIRST MOTHER)

I'm sewing on new buttons
to this washed silk shirt.
Mother-of-pearl,
I chose them carefully.
In the haberdashers on Chepstow Place
I turned a boxful over
one by one,
searching for the backs with flaws:
those blemished green or pink or aubergine,
small birthmarks on the creamy shell.

These afternoons are short,
the sunlight buried after three or four,
sap in the cold earth.
The trees are bare.
I'm six days late.
My right breast aches so
when I bend to catch a fallen button
that strays across the floor.
Either way,
there'll be blood on my hands.

Thirty-seven years ago you sat in poor light
and sewed your time away,
then left.
But I'm no good at this:
a peony of blood gathers on my thumb, falls
then widens on the shirt like a tiny, opening mouth.

I think of you like this –
as darkness comes,
as the window that I can't see through
is veiled with mist

which turns to condensation
slipping down tall panes of glass,
a mirror to the rain outside –
and I know that I'll not know
if you still are mending in the failing light,
or if your hands (as small as mine)
lie still now, clasped together, underground.

Dennis O'Driscoll

FAITH, HOPE, LOSS

1. I stumble on you, prostrate by the door, flat out in a frenzied search for a dropped ear-ring or stone, as if vowing to reform your life in exchange for the recovery of the trinket.

2. With mounting helplessness and rage, my route is retraced in my mind, until I suspect it was in the airport phone booth that I left the missing bag.

3. Losing a loved one. Seeing a daughter eviscerated by cancer, her kindly discoloured face beneath the numbered hairs.

4. To be one of the world's 5.7 billion people: reaching climax, anaesthetised with blockbusters and booze, delving in bins for found art, discarded food. Or one of the three unique species annihilated every hour as grasslands, open-cast mines, weekend shacks impinge.

5. The ditch of lisping water laced with greens, awash with swaying tendrils, dunked leaves, is cemented over; spring light of primroses extinguished; slashed briars where a robin summed up April dusks.

6. Bliss consists of the smallest things. The bus already there to meet the all-night train. Unhappiness lies in what we miss.

7. You are on your knees, convinced that what seems irredeemably lost continues to exist, keeping faith that – given time and patience – it will be restored.

Don Paterson

A Private Bottling

*So I will go, then. I would rather grieve over your absence
than over you.*

Antonio Porchia

Back in the same room that an hour ago
we had led, lamp by lamp, into the darkness
I sit down and turn the radio on low
as the last girl on the planet still awake
reads a dedication to the ships
and puts on a recording of the ocean.

I carefully arrange a chain of nips
in a big fairy-ring; in each square glass
the tincture of a failed geography,
its dwindled burns and woodlands, whin-fires, heather,
the sklent of its wind and its salty rain,
the love-worn habits of its working-folk,
the waveform of their speech, and by extension
how they sing, make love, or take a joke.

So I have a good nose for this sort of thing.

Then I will suffer kiss after fierce kiss
letting their gold tongues slide along my tongue
as each gives up, in turn, its little song
of the patient years in glass and sherry-oak,
the shy negotiations with the sea,
air and earth, the trick of how the peat-smoke
was shut inside it, like a black thought.

Tonight I toast her with the extinct malts
of Ardlussa, Ladyburn and Dalintober
and an ancient pledge of passionate indifference:
Ochon o do dhóigh mé mo chlairsach ar a shon,
wishing her health, as I might wish her weather.

When the circle is closed and I have drunk myself sober
I will tilt the blinds a few degrees, and watch
the dawn grow in a glass of liver-salts,
wait for the birds, the milk-float's sweet nothings,
then slip back to the bed where she lies curled,
replace the live egg of her burning ass
gently, in the cold nest of my lap,
as dead to her as she is to the world.

                              *

Here we are again; it is precisely
twelve, fifteen, thirty years down the road
and one turn higher up the spiral chamber
that separates the burnt ale and dark grains
of what I know, from what I can remember.
Now each glass holds its micro-episode
in permanent suspension, like a movie-frame
on acetate, until it plays again,
revivified by a suave connoisseurship
that deepens in the silence and the dark
to something like an infinite sensitivity.
This is no romantic fantasy: my father
used to know a man who'd taste the sea,
then leave his nets strung out along the bay
because there were no fish in it that day.
Everything is in everything else. It is a matter
of attunement, as once, through the hiss and backwash,
I steered the dial into the voice of God

slightly to the left of Hilversum,
half-drowned by some big, blurry waltz
the way some stars obscure their dwarf companions
for centuries, till someone thinks to look.

In the same way, I can isolate the feints
of feminine effluvia, carrion, shite,
those rogues and toxins only introduced
to give the composition a little weight
as rough harmonics do the violin-note
or Pluto, Cheiron and the lesser saints
might do to our lives, for all you know.
(By Christ, you would recognise their absence
as anyone would testify, having sunk
a glass of *North British*, run off a patent still
in some sleet-hammered satellite of Edinburgh:
a bleak spirit, no amount of caramel
could sweeten or disguise, its after-effect
somewhere between a blanket-bath and a sad wank.
There is, no doubt, a bar in Lothian
where it is sworn upon and swallowed neat
by furloughed riggers and the Special Police,
men who hate the company of women.)

O whiskies of Long Island and Provence!
This little number catches at the throat
but is all sweetness in the finish: my tongue trips
first through burning brake-fluid, then nicotine,
pastis, *Diorissimo* and wet grass;
another is silk sleeves and lip-service
with a kick like a smacked puss in a train-station;
another, the light charge and the trace of zinc
tap-water picks up at the moon's eclipse.
You will know the time I mean by this.

Because your singular absence, in your absence,
has bred hard, tonight I take the waters
with the whole clan: our faceless ushers, bridesmaids,
our four Shelties, three now ghosts of ghosts;
our douce sons and our lovely loudmouthed daughters
who will, by this late hour, be fully grown,
perhaps with unborn children of their own.
So finally, let me propose a toast:
not to love, or life, or real feeling,
but to their sentimental residue;
to your sweet memory, but not to you.

The sun will close its circle in the sky
before I close my own, and drain the purely
offertory glass that tastes of nothing
but silence, burnt dust on the valves, and whisky.

Brian Patten

THE ARMADA

Long long ago
when everything I was told was believable
and the little I knew was less limited than now,
I stretched belly down on the grass beside a pond
and to the far bank launched a child's armada.
    A broken fortress of twigs,
the paper-tissue sails of galleons,
the waterlogged branches of submarines –
all came to ruin and were on flame
in that dusk-red pond.
And you, mother, stood behind me,
impatient to be going,
old at twenty-three, alone,
thin overcoat flapping.
    How closely the past shadows us.
In a hospital a mile or so from that pond
I kneel beside your bed and, closing my eyes,
reach out across forty years to touch once more
that pond's cool surface,
and it is your cool skin I'm touching;
for as on a pond a child's paper boat
was blown out of reach
by the smallest gust of wind,
so too have you been blown out of reach
by the smallest whisper of death,
and a childhood memory is sharpened,
and the heart burns as that armada burnt,
long, long ago.

Katrina Porteous

WRECKED CREEVES

When I see lobster pots the sea has mangled,
The bow-sticks smashed like ribs, the covers tangled
Like wild hair round the lats, the strops all frayed,
It's not the wasting sea I think of, but the men who made them.

Whose hedge-knife stripped these ash sticks in the plantin?
His sea-boot bent each bow till, green and pliant,
Its arch sprang in his arms. Whose fingers, weaving
Strong knots, braided this net one firelit evening?

He hammered home the wedges, and his arm
Beat like a blacksmith's on the stubborn frame;
Deft, then, he intricately stitched inside
With a surgeon's delicacy and a master's eye.

Last week I found a plank stamped R.D.B.
He's dead. But Robbie's creeves still fish this sea
For other men, till east winds and spring tides
Return his broken sticks to the countryside.

There, on the live green grass above the beach,
They're strewn like human bones, worm-riddled, bleached;
And in the warm noon sunshine, bright with larks,
They say, 'Yon sea is caa'd, an' aa'ful dark.'

lats: cross-wise planks on pot's base; *strops:* ropes attached to pots;
plantin: plantation.

Peter Porter

The Western Canoe

We are all in it together, paddling downstream
as in that clip from *Sanders of the River*
but with no one around to shout 'Come on Balliol!'

Undoubtedly here's history in the Steiner sense,
so late into creativity that commentary
gets the prizes, the sexy must be lecturing.

And Bloom's great gun booms heartily
making up for all those snubs, and if he seems
a kosher butcher, at least he's not the Theory Fairy.

In truth, this is a well-equipped canoe,
brother to the Gulf War one, and as attrition
weakens Gibbon, the crew is laser-limning history.

Films are shown on board: *Sophocles' National Service,*
Pico and Vico at the Deux Magots,
Alkan the Alien – but what's so terribly difficult

is starting up afresh. How did they do it, Emily
and friends, out there in the sticks, knowing that a gang
of snobs and clerics had turned the signposts round?

Bliss in that dawn! And if our dawns are chemical
some things never change – a Suburban Sports Reporter
enjoys the engine capacity of a Dickens.

As the canoe beats the rapids to enter the vast
waters of the Eco Pool, drums are calling
for a TV war replete with ice and orphans.

Dangers of shoals and drifting debris, reading habits
Of electronic shoppers – and for the academically-inclined
dropping buoys off in The Swamp of Likenesses.

It reminds us of Maurice Bowra cruising the Aegean –
Daphnis and Chloe country for the educated –
and what are our lives but a narrative of metaphor?

Approaching us, a war canoe half The Lady Murasaki,
half state-of-the-art modem, and in a dream
the 'Waratah' still on her maiden voyage.

Hot in headphones, brushing off the monkeys,
Mr Kurtz hears what the King of Brobdingnag
told Gulliver. He'll reappear upriver.

Peter Redgrove

RELAXATION EXERCISES

I.
Being half-hypnotised
By his caressing mode
By his austere yet rosebud mouth,
Desiring to kiss the dentist,
To pluck the dangerous shiny instruments
From his weakling fingers,

II.
To nestle him down on my lap
Like a great injured bird
In his white coat,
To comfort him in his vast chair
That reclines to take us both
As into one narrow bed.

III.
The Lady Judge
Suckles her child asleep
Without recessing the court,
Parting her scarlet garments,
Doffing her weary wig,
Shaking her own fair soft hair out.

IV.
He eats off plates of museum age,
He sleeps where a hundred
Uncles have slept. My pious
Cousin loosens his britches
And shows me his Thing
Shining with grace. I am full
Of admiration, so my own
Thing shines, nearly

As bright as his.
The old house is dimly lit
By the soft shining of our Things
And by the ancient lamps
Brought over from Gwythion.

V.
Dogface, devoted,
Dedicated, looks
About it and becomes
Everything, wees
Its passion against
A cherry-tree trunk, does
Its doke, squeezes
Its stuff, circling, while
The doleful brown
Eyes stare deeply inwards.
He is in his dog-trance and,
If praised, will follow the praiser
Everywhere.

VI.
A knot in the thorn-bough
Like a head of Christ
Carved in the tree
By the tree.

VII.
My bucking stomach, my lurching heart,
The old broken shed twined with honeysuckle;
The more I throw up
The clearer and more beautiful
The honeysuckle becomes;
The more filth I shoot over its roots
The more piercing

The fragrance of the honeysuckle;
As I empty myself shuddering
The more my kinship
With these flowering flames and shattered shed.

VIII.
Certain caves
Of the body must be emptied:
The armpits, the groin's
Inner oxters, the diaphragm's
Echoing chamber, the swishing
Park of the lungs, the elasticated
Spinal muscles; the breath will now
Ooze through the chest-skin, the body
Shrink like a discarded twig, and the head
Dwindle to a stop.

IX.
The yellow yacht
Of the millionaire
Who is seen only in summer;
Sailors sleep among the sails,
Young sailors,
As birds sleep among their wings.

X.
The leaves step out suddenly
Like hurrying footprints
All green and sighing, and the tree
Is speedily full
Of birds new-hatched, egg-wet,
And singing as if cool water
Boiled.

XI.
The canvas is laid out
In the sailmaker's field
Like the stained underwear
Of a sleeping giantess.

XII.
See the dry
Cunts of the statues,
Their parched eyes,
Their sandy robes; and see
How in the rain the statues shine,
Putter and shine.

XIII.
He offers her
The glittering cigarette-case of the Great Ziegfeld;
She replies
'My breasts
Are under the protection of God and His mermaids!'
But his hands
Are wonderful, like pearl, he
Touches me up in an accurate style
Which suggests that I am actually a mermaid;
And the form of my personal fishpool
Was entirely familiar to him.

XIV.
Fitting fresh words to the spring's
Water-table talk.

Eva Salzman

Trepanned

Bad enough, not to have trekked the Himalayas
or smoked a pipe in the back of a Volkswagen bus
with Storm the mechanic, who, with blessings from us
changed the oil and filter en route to enlightenment.
Let's just say you were part of my dimmer days;
I turned the lights down low to cosmic bliss,
laughed at the spirit, in spirits, excited the men.
A corporeal slant. And all I wanted was this:

one little plastic piece of that five-and-dime belief,
a novelty axe to hack at the totems of numbers
on your PC screen. I wanted hand relief –
that is, the gentle touch just before you go under.
Nothing profound, nothing deep. Which is why
I let you drill that Black and Decker into my third eye.

Ruth Silcock

THE ELOCUTION LESSON

'Feel me breathe, girls,' –
Miss Bannerman places
Our pink open hands
On her emerald dress.

She presses our palms
Across thick, crinkly wool,
Our fingers extend
Along muscles and ribs.

'In – Out, In – Out,'
Miss Bannerman breathes,
Her bony chest heaves,
In – Out go our hands.

Our hands are pink fans
That Miss Bannerman breathes
Into movement, *In – Out*,
By the strength of her ribs.

Miss Bannerman's hair
Is a bright wavy brown,
Her lips are bright red,
Her body bright green,

Her eyes dark and sad,
Her thin ribs alive –
One by one, we draw back
While Miss Bannerman breathes.

Benjamin Zephaniah

The Angry Black Poet

Next on stage
The have the angry black poet,
So angry
He won't allow himself to fall in luv,
So militant
You will want to see him again.
Don't get me wrong
He means it,
He means it so much
He is unable to feel,
He's so serious
If he is found smiling
He stops to get serious before he enters stage left,
Through days he dreams of freedom
Through nights he rants of freedom,
Tonight he will speak for you,
Give him a hand.

Please give him a hand,
Help him,
He too has silent moments
He could do without,
I have worked with him
And I know
He needs stroking
He needs to play
Let him know you are there.

I knew him when he was unknown
I knew him when he was happy,
Now he's angry
You will luv him,
He lives on the edge

He has highs and lows,
And I know
He hates publicity
And he luvs you all,
Be quiet
And let's hear it for
The angry black poet.